# What People Are Saying

After twenty-eight years of marriage, I was clueless about how to introduce myself as a newly single woman. I was afraid of the unknown and when I asked the few acquaintances I had who were also divorced, I soon discovered that most of them were scared, stuck, and clueless, too!

Not only did Dee give me hope that I really could live happily as a single woman, she gave me tons of support as I looked at all my choices and specific "how tos" as the "what ifs" occurred to me. I can't thank Dee enough for the information and inspiration she gave me during a very difficult time in my life.

—Julie Overholt, professional certified coach

Dee Frazier truly is "The Dating Diva"! Her wisdom, attitude, and sense of humor in her book have helped me "lighten up" while reentering the single world after my divorce! Thanks to Dee, for the first time in my adult life, I am having so much fun dating again!

—Laura Lewis, CCN, author of *52 Ways to Live a Long and Healthy Life*

I thought, initially, that I might not hear anything I hadn't heard or read before, so I was skeptical at best, but willing. I know I have grown as a person. I notice a self-confidence about me and a lack of uneasiness about what to do, which, before, has kept me from meeting others. I keep smiling, no matter what, and the biggest change is that I'm making eye contact and seeing positive reactions. That sounds pretty simple to some, but for me, it's such an improvement.

—Onna Seibold, workshop attendee

Very enjoyable. The workshop really helped me come out with a fresher, more fun-loving approach to dating. "I'm having lots of fun dates!"

—Art H, workshop attendee

Dee is an incredibly dynamic woman who has been successful in many different areas of life. Her dating and relating advice comes from her personal experience, her knowledge as a business and life coach, and most especially from her deep wisdom and caring. She has been an exceptional coach and mentor.

—Fran Assaf, DC

Dating 101 is a delightful book filled with practical tips that are needed when one finds one's self thrust into the single world. It treats the experience of dating with warmth, love, and discovery. Her book takes being single back into basic relating from the heart. Fear of dating dissolves as the reader connects with the real, spontaneous, and authentic part of himself or herself. Definitely this book is a must read for anyone who wants to "lighten up" and play.

—Barbara Graham, PhD, spiritual psychologist and author of *Healing Sacred Wounds: Forgiving from the Heart of Compassion; Journey to Forgiveness* and *A Transpersonal Manual on Forgiveness*

# Dating 101

*Dear Cassie~
Create the
loving life
that you love~
to live

Love)
Dee*

# Dating 101

## The Second, Third, or Fourth Time Around

### By Deanna Frazier
#### "Dee, the Dating Diva"

**BROWN BOOKS**

## Dating 101: The Second, Third, or Fourth Time Around

© 2005 Deanna Frazier

All rights reserved. No part of this publication may be reproduced, stored in any retrieval system, or transmitted in any form or by any means, mechanical, photocopying, recording, or otherwise, without permission in writing from the publisher, except by a reviewer, who may quote brief passages in a review to be printed in a magazine or newspaper.

Manufactured in the United States of America.

For information, please contact:
Brown Books Publishing Group
16200 North Dallas Parkway, Suite 170
Dallas, Texas 75248
www.brownbooks.com
972-381-0009
*A New Era in Publishing*™

ISBN 1-933285-18-4
LCCN 2005908781
10 9 8 7 6 5 4 3 2 1

# Table of Contents

Preface: Why and for Whom Was This Book Written ............................ xi

Introduction: How I Got in the Dating Coach Business ........................ xiii

The Guiding Principles ............................................................ xv

Part 1: Getting Ready to Get Ready ............................................... 1

1  Choose to Change ............................................................... 2

2  Delete Your Old Programming .............................................. 5

3  Notice the Stories You Tell Yourself ...................................... 8

4  Forgive ............................................................................. 10

5  Develop Confidence through Courage .................................. 13

6  Realize Where You Exist ..................................................... 15

7  Learn Self-acceptance ........................................................ 18

8  Dump the Excuses for Not Getting Out ................................. 20

9  Avoid the Couch ................................................................ 23

10  Absolutely Avoid the Pity Party ........................................... 25

11  Practice Extreme Self-care .................................................. 27

12  Stop Asking, "Am I Too Old for This Stuff?" ......................... 30

13  Stop Gender Bashing .......................................................... 32

14  Get Rid of Guilt ................................................................. 34

15  Have Fun While You Are in Therapy ................................... 37

16  Unclutter Your Life ............................................................ 39

# Dating 101

**Part 2: Diving In** .................................................................... 43
  1 Go for What You Want ............................................... 44
  2 Let Go of the Ego ........................................................ 46
  3 Shine Your Light .......................................................... 50
  4 Be a Star ........................................................................ 52
  5 Become Passionate ...................................................... 54
  6 Be the Kind of Date That You Want to Have ......... 57
  7 Be Happy and Content with Yourself and Your Life .... 61
  8 Ask Yourself if You Are Seeing Clearly ................... 63
  9 Remember, First Dates Are Just a Moment in Time .... 67
  10 Stop the Buzzing in Your Brain ................................ 69
  11 Be Authentic and Honest ........................................... 71
  12 Do Not Take Rejection Personally ........................... 73
  13 Conquer Fear of Rejection ......................................... 75
  14 Design Your New Wardrobe ..................................... 77
  15 Direct Your New Healthy Lifestyle .......................... 81
  16 Let Your Friends Help ................................................ 84

**Part 3: Learning Dating Tactics** ......................................... 89
  1 Have Fun with Flirting! .............................................. 90

# Table of Contents

| | | |
|---|---|---|
| 2 | Take Cues | 93 |
| 3 | Be Careful with Your Opinions | 95 |
| 4 | Avoid Mind Reading | 97 |
| 5 | Be Approachable | 102 |
| 6 | Dance Your Way to New Friends and Fitness | 104 |
| 7 | Do Have a Quick Comeback | 106 |
| 8 | Know Who Pays | 108 |
| 9 | Log in to Ads, Dating Services, and Singles Clubs | 110 |
| 10 | Keep the Spark . . . Be in the Moment | 113 |
| 11 | Be Fully Yourself | 115 |
| 12 | Get Seen, Get Heard | 117 |
| 13 | Be Persistent | 119 |
| 14 | Develop a Thick, Yet Removable, Skin | 121 |
| 15 | Emulate the Greatest (to a Point) | 123 |
| 16 | Entertain Yourself | 125 |
| 17 | Build a Community | 127 |
| 18 | Think of the Date as an Interview . . . Sort Of | 129 |
| 19 | Use the Magic of "No" | 133 |
| 20 | Accept Compliments | 135 |

## Dating 101

| 21 | Be Playful | 137 |
| 22 | Look for Friends, Not Lovers | 139 |
| 23 | Decide Where to Go | 141 |
| 24 | Invite a Friend | 144 |
| 25 | Learn and Practice Etiquette | 146 |
| 26 | Dos and Don'ts on the First Date | 148 |
| 27 | Consider These Dos and Don'ts of the First Date | 150 |
| 28 | Things to Avoid if You Want a Second Date | 153 |

Part 4: Last-Minute "Tools" for Your Dating Toolbox ... 157

| 1 | Understand Acceptable Flattery Zones | 158 |
| 2 | Heed the Dating Red Flags | 160 |
| 3 | Dump a Bad Date | 163 |
| 4 | Choose Dates Who Are the Right Age . . . For You | 166 |
| 5 | Decide Whether or Not to Have Sex | 168 |
| 6 | Knowing What You Are Really Feeling: Is It Love or Just Chemistry? | 171 |
| 7 | Dance | 173 |
| 8 | Deciding Where to Go Next | 175 |

Afterword: Living Happily Ever After ... 177

Acknowledgments ... 183

## Preface

# Why and for Whom This Book Was Written

There are many dating books out there, but the common theme seems to be: "If you do these things, you will find your ultimate relationship, soul mate, or partner for life." Well, that may be so; however, this book is about having a "stunning" relationship with yourself and whatever happens after that . . . happens.

*Dating 101: The Second, Third, or Fourth Time Around,* was written to redefine the dating experience and the experience of being single again—or still—after the age of forty-five. It's about dating and relating to other singles and enjoying life. It's a journey of fun and learning. Most importantly, this book is to remind you that . . .

It's just a date—not the rest of your life!

The grown-up dating game has never been more interesting and challenging. There are more players than ever before. Why? Because of higher divorce rates, longer life spans, and a greater tendency to postpone or skip marriage altogether. These factors contribute to more single Americans than at any other time in our country's history.

The U.S. Census Bureau tells us that of the 97 million Americans who are forty-five or older, almost 40 percent (36.2 million) are available singles. There is no shame in being single.

## Introduction

# How I Got in the Dating Coach Business

I have been married and divorced three times and proposed to at least three times! And I have spent more years single and on the dating scene than I have spent married. I have personally participated in almost every type of dating experience—good and bad—including long-distance relationships, phone relationships, online relationships, short and long relationships, friendships, codependent relationships . . . You name it, I've tried it.

I spent the seventeen years after my last divorce healing, learning, and growing into someone who enjoys life. These years have given me multitudes of personal experiences to share, as well as the collective experiences of all of the friends, clients, and seminar participants that I have had the good fortune to coach in the last decade. I believe that being single is challenging, and at the same time, wonderful. I have given advice to many people as they bravely enter back into the world of dating. Several of my clients have referred to my advice as "Dating Survival Tactics."

## Dating 101

I am a certified coach and have, for the past thirty years, delivered seminars, training, and coaching to men and women from all walks of life. I have been a catalyst for people who choose to transform through their own wisdom. I teach those individuals to promote themselves and be positive. I was recently spotlighted on a nationally syndicated television show called *Smart Woman* as a dating expert. During the show, I delivered real-time coaching to audience participants.

My purpose in life is to support and coach other people in achieving happiness through accepting themselves, their sexuality, and their desire to have a healthy, happy, single life. I have coached many single friends, clients, and seminar attendees on how to prepare for reentry into the dating world and how to love having fun as a single person.

Over the years, many of my friends and clients have encouraged me to write and speak about dating and becoming irresistibly attractive. After ignoring these well-wishers for a while, one day a friend at a party introduced me as "Dee, the Dating Diva," and I knew it was time . . . the University of Dating was founded.

# The Guiding Principles

As you read the following pages, keep in mind these three fundamental ideas:

*The University of Dating is in the business of redefining the dating experience.*

*Dating is fun and not a means to an end. It's about dating, not about mating.*

*It's just a date—not the rest of your life!*

**Part 1: Getting Ready to Get Ready**

# Part 1: Getting Ready to Get Ready

# 1
# Choose to Change

*One change makes way for the next,
giving us opportunity to grow.*

## —Vivian Buchen

# Part 1: Getting Ready to Get Ready

Change! Change what?! I know that you are already thinking—no way. Let me say it clearly: you will have to. You will change your thinking, your beliefs, your dress, your perceptions, your assumptions, your opinions, your communications skills, and anything else that isn't working in your life right now. Anything that is preventing you from getting what you want in this world will have to go.

A client who had become single after a twenty-seven-year marriage told me: "I had to face the judgment that I always had towards newly divorced women, especially how they dressed."

When I look back and think about how many changes I have made in my life to get me where I am today, I am amazed. I will tell you this: the older you get, the easier it becomes. You have less to lose. You get to the point where there is nothing left to learn the hard way.

# Dating 101

Life is not a dress rehearsal . . . life is a live performance.

Life IS the event!!

In this book, we will take steps toward helping you create the life that you want to be living right now, today . . . not a life that has just "shown up."

*Life is a smorgasbord, and most poor suckers are starving to death!*
> **—Auntie Mame**

So let the feast begin . . .

## Part 1: Getting Ready to Get Ready

# 2
# Delete Your Old Programming

*Our beliefs about what we are and what we can be precisely determine what we will be.*

—**Anthony Robbins**

# Dating 101

A client of mine named John S. had been married several times and he was again divorced and had been single for several years, but he had not dated at all. When I first asked him why, he said, "Well, I know if I have a date, it will lead to another date, and before you know it I am three months into a relationship and I can't get out."

So I said: "How about dinner from eight to ten? Not the rest of your life."

Here are some questions to ask yourself as you "get ready to get ready" to date again.

1. What are the thoughts and beliefs (the false "I-dentities") that limit your life?

2. What are the ways you run away when you hit your edges?

3. What will help you stop running away and learn to sit still when you hit your edges?

## Part 1: Getting Ready to Get Ready

4. What would help you have the courage to look inside, challenge your beliefs, and live with anxiety, confusion, and discomfort?

Here is a great exercise; do it now.

Close your eyes and imagine that you have no emotional baggage, that you have never been hurt in any of your relationships—not by your mother, your father, or by anyone else. Imagine that you can trust everyone in your life, including yourself, to do what is right for you. Close your eyes and do that now . . . really imagine it.

Now see yourself deleting negative memories from your past but keeping any learning or lessons. Create an irresistible smile on your face. People will remember your smile.

This mantra was taught to me by a wonderful therapist and it really works: "I am the best of both of my parents."

Dating 101

# 3
# Notice the Stories You Tell Yourself

*I never cease being dumfounded by the unbelievable things people believe.*

—**Leo Rosten**

## Part 1: Getting Ready to Get Ready

The fears about dating are born in the stories we tell ourselves. We experienced a troublesome event, we had an emotional response, and then we created a story to explain it to alleviate our pain. Over time, we repeated the story until it took on a life of its own and started to become a script we followed.

I heard a wonderful talk by Don Miguel Ruiz, the author of *The Four Agreements*. He referred to the movie *A Beautiful Mind* and the plight of John Nash, who is a schizophrenic. As John Nash's disease escalated, he was creating a life of horror based on visions, images, and voices that were actually lies caused by his disease.

Mr. Ruiz somewhat jokingly referred to his audience once, and said we are all somewhat schizophrenic because we live lives based on lies we tell ourselves. Even if we don't see things, we certainly hear them . . . voices in the back of our mind that tell us what's wrong with us and what's wrong with everything else out there.

Dating 101

# 4
# Forgive

*Forgiveness is not an elective in the curriculum of life. It is a required course, and the exams are always tough to pass.*

**— Charles Swindoll**

# Part 1: Getting Ready to Get Ready

Forgiveness is an act of the imagination. It dares you to imagine a better future, one that is based on the blessed possibility that your hurt will not be the final word on the matter. It challenges you to give up your destructive thoughts about the situation and to believe in the possibility of a better future. It builds confidence that you can survive the pain and grow from it.

*Forgiveness is the fragrance the violet sheds on the heel that has crushed it.*

—**Mark Twain**

# Dating 101

In one of my workshops not that long ago, a woman mentioned that men were not trustworthy. After her longtime marriage ended in divorce, she had a relationship pretty quickly, and for whatever reason, she determined that the new man was not trustworthy. He may not have been. I don't know, but I do know that her inability to forgive her husband, her relationship, and herself kept her saying that all men were not trustworthy. She hadn't had a date in a long time, and hooray, she signed up for my dating workshop.

Pretty soon she was able to make a shift in that "story" and begin to have some fun.

I work on this all the time. It's a life process. Here is an affirmation that is great to say to yourself before you go to bed: "I forgive the world; the world forgives me; I forgive myself." The most important person to forgive is yourself.

Part 1: Getting Ready to Get Ready

# 5
# Develop Confidence through Courage

*Courage is not the absence of fear, rather it is the ability to take action in the face of fear.*

—**Nancy Anderson**

## Dating 101

Some people will tell you that you need to be more confident. What is confidence, and where do you go to learn it?

Confidence is belief and faith in yourself. How will you get that? By making mistakes, by getting out of the locker room and onto the playing field, and by giving yourself permission to fall down, get back up, dust yourself off, and try again. No one ever died from saying the wrong thing, by going to a cocktail party in the wrong outfit because she didn't read the invitation, or even by saying "yes" when he knew he should have said "no."

I make those mistakes a lot less now, but once in a while when I reflect, I say, "Darn, that was a mistake." Oh well. Onward and forward.

*You become what you believe—not what you wish or want, but what you truly believe. Wherever you are in life, look at your beliefs. They put you there!*

**—Oprah**

*Overcoming fear and worry can be accomplished by living a day at a time or even a moment at a time. Your worries will be cut down to nothing.*

**—Robert Anthony**

Part 1: Getting Ready to Get Ready

# 6

# Realize Where You Exist

*Realize deeply that the present moment is all you ever have. Make the now the primary focus of life. Whereas before you dwelt in time and paid brief visits to the now, have your dwelling place in the now and pay brief visits to the past and future when required to deal with the practical aspects of your life situation.*

**—Eckhart Tolle, *The Power of Now***

# Dating 101

Do you remember *Star Trek?* One of their series, *Deep Space Nine,* was profound. The new captain entered into a place where the entities had the ability to read his mind. As they probed his mind they would ask him questions that would take him to different points in his life. For a while, he actually thought he was reliving those moments.

The captain became frustrated as he continually flashed back to the time of his wife's tragic death. The aliens constantly said, "You exist here." He tried to explain that he was captain of a space station. The aliens proclaimed, "But you exist here!" He finally got the message. He existed in his past. He had never moved past the tragedy that happened years ago. The aliens' honesty only put him where his mind was all the time.

## Part 1: Getting Ready to Get Ready

Your existence lies deep within your subconscious mind. If your focus is on the past, then you cannot operate in the present. The captain knew he could not lead a space station if all his mental energy were focused on a past tragedy. Your past is good to learn from, not to dwell on.

Are you existing in your past, or focusing on your future? We all have made mistakes. Don't beat yourself up for making them. I have not met anyone without some past hurt or issue. Your true happiness will be determined by your ability to stop existing in the past and to start stepping toward your future.

Dating 101

# 7
# Learn Self-acceptance

*History is full of incompetent people who were beloved, blunderers with winsome personality traits, and inept folks who delighted their entourage with their unassuming presences. Their secret? To accept their flaws with the same grace and humility as their best qualities.*

—**Veronique Vienne, *The Art of Imperfection***

## Part 1: Getting Ready to Get Ready

Confidence comes with self-acceptance. No more excuses about who you are and what you have done. I am here, and I am glad and proud to be who I am.

> *Until I accept my faults I will most certainly doubt my virtues.*
>
> **—Hugh Prather**

Oh, by the way—being self-assured and self-confident is very SEXY!

Dating 101

# 8

# Dump the Excuses for Not Getting Out

*One excuse is as good as another.*

—**Everyone**

## Part 1: Getting Ready to Get Ready

Sticks and stones may break our bones, but words will break our hearts.

Aren't you sick of saying the same old thing, anyway?

Ask yourself if you recognize these old excuses:

- I'm too busy.

- I'm waiting for the right person.

- The good ones are all married.

- All men/women are jerks.

- I'm shy. (There are a lot of shy married people—they dated too.)

- I can't do this to the children.

# Dating 101

- They're all losers . . . or am I?
- It's going to be a disaster.
- I'm not ready.
- No one will like me.
- I've been hurt too many times before.

Can you imagine if a baby decided not to get up every time he fell down while he was learning to walk?

Let me be the first to tell you, you won't always do it right. So WHAT!?

If you don't take a stand, you won't stand a chance!!

Part 1: Getting Ready to Get Ready

# 9

# Avoid the Couch

*You don't have just one chance to win, but you don't have unlimited opportunities either.*

**—Anonymous**

## Dating 101

You know that the fact is, nobody knocks on your door and asks you for a date . . . well, unless you have neighbors in the same circumstances. But for the most part, nothing will happen unless you make it happen. Get off the couch and into life. I know it's not easy, but once you try, it becomes easier. You will be amazed at what you find out there: yourself!

Your couch will appreciate your getting off it as well. If the groove in your couch seems permanent, the couch is tired. However, it may be all right for some snuggling with someone, so don't throw it out.

**Part 1: Getting Ready to Get Ready**

# 10
# Absolutely Avoid the Pity Party

*Eliminating self-pity allows self-respect to return.*

**—Anonymous**

## Dating 101

This party can be held with one or more people. Avoid it like the plague. There is no fun at these parties, and, in fact, they become almost addictive. The more you have them, the more you need them. Getting out is really difficult if you have a lot of self-pity going on. Self-pity leads to self-loathing, and self-loathing leads to . . . Need I say more?

The only sure weapons against self-pity are awareness, understanding, and a healthy sense of humor. You must learn to recognize the pity party each time it charges down on you. If life's pressure is closing in on you, if one more difficult or impossible demand is made on you . . . enter self-pity. "Poor me! Why did this happen to me? Why am I single?" Stop the party!

*If you could really accept that you weren't OK,*
*you could stop proving you were OK.*
*If you could stop proving that you were OK,*
*You could get that it was OK not to be OK.*
*If you could get that it was OK not to be OK,*
*You could get that you were OK the way you are. You're OK, get it?*

—**Werner Erhard**

Part 1: Getting Ready to Get Ready

# 11

# Practice Extreme Self-care

*How would your life be different if you learned how to love and respect your body as though it were your own precious creation, as valuable as a beloved friend or child? How would you treat yourself differently?*

**—Christiane Northrup, MD**

# Dating 101

Here's a little checklist to help remind you of the kinds of things that might need your attention. As you read over the list, notice which items spark an "I've been meaning to get that one" response.

1. Do you need to have a complete physical?

2. When was the last time you had an eye exam?

3. Is a trip to the dentist in order?

4. How's your back? Have you been meaning to see a chiropractor or make an appointment with a massage therapist?

## Part 1: Getting Ready to Get Ready

5. Have you ever had a manicure or pedicure? After all, stop to consider how much work your hands and feet do to support you!

6. How about a facial? Although a facial may seem like a luxury, as you get older, you'll be glad that you've taken good care of your face.

7. Are you happy with your hairstyle?

These are just some of the examples of the basic body care areas that can make a big difference in how you feel.

Dating 101

# 12

# Stop Asking, "Am I Too Old for This Stuff?"

*People don't grow old. When they stop growing, they become old.*

—**Anonymous**

# Part 1: Getting Ready to Get Ready

*We don't stop playing because we grow old; we grow old because we stop playing.*

**—George Bernard Shaw**

*There is a fountain of youth: it is your mind, your talents, the creativity you bring to your life and the lives of people you love. When you learn to tap this source, you will truly have defeated age.*

**—Sophia Loren**

Need I say more? Life really does begin after forty-five!

Dating 101

# 13

# Stop Gender Bashing

*Talking about your grievances merely adds to those grievances. Give recognition only to what you desire.*

—**Thomas Dreier**

## Part 1: Getting Ready to Get Ready

If you have ever been with anyone who spends most of his or her time bashing a former mate or the opposite sex in general, you know how tiresome and disgusting the conversation can be. It leads nowhere and is depressing. If you have the state of mind that the opposite sex "did you wrong," it will probably keep you immobilized and unable to have fun as a single person. Keep yourself from saying those things and eventually you will stop thinking them.

**Dating 101**

# 14

# Get Rid of Guilt

*Mistakes are part of the dues one pays for a full life.*

**—Sophia Loren**

## Part 1: Getting Ready to Get Ready

It is no surprise that guilt is at the top of the list when talking about self-care. Guilt is the most common obstacle that prevents people from making choices that will improve the quality of their lives. If you're someone who is used to putting the needs of others before your own, there's a good chance that you'll feel guilty when you begin to put your self-care at the top of your "to-do" list. It's a natural response to this new behavior.

Too often we try to deal with guilt by telling ourselves to stop feeling that way. Telling yourself to stop feeling guilty is like telling a friend to stop feeling nervous before she goes on her first date. It just doesn't work. Instead, you'll need to understand what drives the guilt so you can begin to respond to it in a different way.

## Dating 101

Feelings of guilt can be linked to having low self-esteem. For example, when you continuously give to others at the expense of yourself, you're making a statement that says their needs are more valuable than yours. When you value the needs of others over your own, your self-esteem is certain to suffer. This creates a vicious cycle—the less I value myself, the less worthy I feel of having my needs met, and the more I continue to put the needs of others before my own.

Practicing extreme self-care will break this cycle. But in order to put your self-care first, you'll need to spend some time learning how to become desensitized to your conditioned feelings of guilt. Once you do, you'll find yourself having these feelings less often and less intensely.

Part 1: Getting Ready to Get Ready

# 15
# Have Fun While You Are in Therapy

*A good hearty laugh is worth ten thousand "groans" and a million "sighs" in any market on earth.*

**—Napoleon Hill**

## Dating 101

Impossible, you say? Not really. For many people, therapy—after a breakup, death, or for whatever reason—is very appropriate, but it doesn't mean that you have to stop your life while you are going through that process. In fact, healthy play is healthy and healing.

One of the special gifts my therapist of years ago told me was that I was really blessed because no matter how hard things were, I could always play.

**Part 1: Getting Ready to Get Ready**

# 16

# Unclutter Your Life

*The clutter on the outside represents the clutter inside.*

—**Dee Frazier**

## Dating 101

Sometimes we dating and life coaches will find humor in the fact that one of the first things we tell clients is to "clean out their clutter" so they start with their closets, feel better, and think we are wonderful.

Clutter isn't only physical. Mental and emotional clutter can keep you from doing what you really want to do. Here are some tips for "unloading" the clutter in your life. It's time for spring cleaning!

1. Get rid of the human vampires. Avoid contact with people who are energy drains. Even if they're family members who you can't avoid altogether, make a decision to limit the time you are around them, and to choose issues in which you will allow them to engage you.

2. Learn to say NO. It's the first word you learned as a toddler. Use it! It's your lifetime resource and you have the right to use it as you see fit, without comments from the peanut gallery.

## Part 1: Getting Ready to Get Ready

3. Take time for YOU. Time is short for all of us. Make a decision to set aside downtime that is just for you, even if you can only start with fifteen minutes a day. Lock the door, turn off the phone, do it.

4. Have a garage or sidewalk sale. Getting rid of physical stuff you don't need frees you up mentally and physically.

5. Pay cash. Credit card bills equal bondage and lack of freedom. Free yourself and create choices for the things that really matter to you. If you can't pay for it, you don't need it.

6. Limit tradition. Most tradition is senseless and wastes time. If it doesn't make sense, forget it!

7. Embrace quality time. Schedule time for the special people in your life and then FOCUS only on them without distractions. You will both enjoy your time together more if you know beforehand that nothing else will get in the way.

# Dating 101

8. Forget the Joneses. Even if you believe everyone's watching you, the truth is no one's paying that much attention to you.

9. Live YOUR life.

What works for someone else may not work for you. Take direction from your inner instinct and go with it!

Think about applying Einstein's three rules of work to your dating life:

1. Out of clutter find simplicity.

2. From discord find harmony.

3. In the middle of difficulty lies opportunity.

# Part 2:
# Diving In

Dating 101

# 1

# Go for What You Want

*A total commitment is paramount to reaching the ultimate in performance.*

**—Tom Flores**

## Part 2: Diving In

S till going strong? Who would have believed it? You thought it would be all over by the time you hit forty-five. The good looks and the vitality and the passion would be over.

I sometimes joke that if you light all the candles on my birthday cake, it will set off the fire alarm. The truth is, the fire is really inside me—it's inside all of us! The bigger the fire, the more difficult it is to put it out.

Look back to where you came from. Enjoy the gained confidence and wisdom. You no longer have to wonder who you are. You KNOW! Now go for what you want and make it big.

The best way I know to tell people to dive in is, "DIVE IN!" Do not wait until you feel certain and sure of yourself. Getting out, dating, mingling, and socializing will make you more certain and self-assured.

# 2

# Let Go of the Ego

*Those who travel the high road of humility . . .
are not troubled by heavy traffic.*

**—Senator Alan K. Simpson**

## Part 2: Diving In

OK fine, now what exactly does this mean? Well, it means that you should be guided by your heart and soul, not your rigid ego.

A healthy ego allows us to let compassion flow in and out. It allows us to have the strength of our convictions, yet to be open to other people and to events and happenings around us.

When we think about "ego strength," we think about assuredness that rests calmly inside, the will to actualize our dreams.

However, the rigid or inflated ego is fixed in concrete. It's black/white, right/wrong, good/bad, and friend/foe. It is tied to past experiences that have become hardwired in the brain, and results in rigid beliefs, fear of change, and an inability to see the many sides of a situation.

## Dating 101

*The rigid ego is worried, urgent and intense, and afraid. It says, "I've got to have someone, I can't stand being alone. There's something wrong with me for being single at this age."*
— **Charlotte Kasl, from *If the Buddha Dated***

In other words, a rigid ego is what keeps us judgmental and negative in beliefs about ourselves and everyone else. If you trust that you will make the right decisions and that you are safe, you will know that you are protected and you can let your guard down and your heart show.

Casting aside your rigid ego means:

- You are willing to be vulnerable.

- You will not manipulate others to get your needs met.

## Part 2: Diving In

- You will not be a victim.

- You do not look outside yourself for something to change so that your life can work. Your success and happiness are not outside yourself.

- You will take your life in your own hands and see what happens. Guess what?! Now there's no one else to blame, since you are responsible for your own life.

Empowerment comes through realizing that you cannot control what happens to you, but you can choose how you will respond to it. Another mantra to repeat to yourself: "Whatever happens, I can handle it; and if I can't, I can handle that."

# 3
# Shine Your Light

*Our deepest fear is not that we are inadequate. Our deepest fear is that we are powerful beyond measure. It is our light, not our darkness that frightens us.*

**—Nelson Mandela**

## Part 2: Diving In

OK, here you go. Lights . . . action . . . roll 'em! The light within you has been turned on, and you are shining from the inside out. Wow, what a picture that makes. That light is a gift we give to everyone we meet. We shine on them and it makes a difference. Nothing has to be said. Suddenly, we are approachable and the reasons don't have to be explained; they are simply known. Shining your own light draws others to you.

Smile and keep smiling. Laugh and keep laughing. Find things that are funny and that make you laugh, like books and movies. You won't find a happy person unless you become happy first.

Unless you develop a strong sense of self, the people who show up for dates will be like you. You want light? BE the light!

Your light is your inner beauty—let it shine through.

Attitude is contagious. It carries energy that fills you up and makes you want to reach higher. Project an air of confidence, intrigue, and sexy fun—in other words, let the true, irresistible YOU radiate.

Oh, and by the way: you can fake it until you make it.

# 4
# Be a Star

*In your life you are the star. Sometimes we forget to shine.*

**—Everyone**

## Part 2: Diving In

Action! You're on! Think of yourself as being in front of a camera, playing the part of your lifetime . . . something that you have been waiting to do for a very long time. You are dressed to the "hilt" in that designer gown or perfectly tailored tux, and you will be giving your ultimate performance. OK, so it's not real yet. Who cares? The fantasy is fun and it's a great way of alleviating any fears before that first date or big social event.

Be the star in your own mind and the message will come through and your admirers will love you.

Have fun with this!

# 5
# Become Passionate

*Your reward for passion is the wonderful way it feels to be passionate, and the incredible things that pour into your life when you are.*

**—Marianne Williamson**

## Part 2: Diving In

**P**assion is not hiding out there somewhere, waiting to be found. Instead, it comes from inside. Developing the ability to recognize and feel passion is necessary in order to experience its power to transform and improve our lives.

Being a passionate person requires enthusiasm.

Enthusiasm is not an emotional state. It is a spiritual commitment, a loving surrender to our creative process, a loving recognition of all the creativity around us.

We sit in the darkened theater with the big screen and state-of-art sound, waiting to see MGM's newly restored print of *Singin' in the Rain*. We watch Gene Kelly throw his head back and holler, "GOTTA DANCE!"

Passion is intense emotional excitement. It's a feeling that comes to those who are intense. It's the fire in the heart . . . the fire in the belly . . . the engagement with something or someone . . . or life itself.

Passion does not only love the outcome, it absolutely loves the process. Passion is the expression of the soul.

Above all, passion is about being free. Contrary to myth, passions don't enslave us; they are fuel that fires our rockets of individuality.

We are most alive when we acknowledge, embrace, and enjoy the things or people we love, whether our passions burn fiercely or glow gently.

Passion enables us to celebrate life more fully and joyously. It can lead us to express our highest good and deepest love and even go beyond the personal to the common welfare.

**Part 2: Diving In**

# 6

# Be the Kind of Date That You Want to Have

*If you want to know what is going on inside of you, look at the people you call friends.*

**—Anonymous**

# Dating 101

I once heard the well-known speaker and author of the best seller *Return to Love*, Marianne Williamson, speak to a large audience about relationships and dating. One of the things she said made a lasting impression on me. She was talking about how, in general, we make lists of the qualities we want in a date. She went on to list the various types of things that people ask for regarding physical qualities, financial requirements, emotional stability, generosity, spirituality, and on and on.

She said that we take this list and we say, "OK, God, send him (or her)." Then she said, "Now really, if this person showed up, would he or she date you!?"

The audience bellowed, but it's true: we ask for something that we are unwilling to be, but the "law of attraction" absolutely says that we have to become what we want.

## Part 2: Diving In

- If you want to be accepted—be accepting.

- If you want to be treated kindly—be kind.

- If you want someone secure in himself or herself—be secure with yourself.

- If you want to attract someone who is in shape and has a healthy lifestyle—be in shape and have a healthy lifestyle.

- If you want to attract good communicators who treat you well—make sure your communication skills are polished, and pay attention to how you treat others.

Who and what we attract into our lives is based on how we see ourselves.

## Dating 101

Let me tell you an old story about three bricklayers:

A visitor walked up to a work site and asked the first bricklayer what he was doing. The bricklayer yawned and said, "I'm laying bricks." The visitor then went to the second bricklayer and asked what he was doing. Patting the brickwork he had completed, the second bricklayer said, "I'm building a wall."

Finally, the visitor came to a third bricklayer who was whistling as he worked, and the visitor asked him what he was doing. The whistling bricklayer smiled and said, "Why, I'm building a cathedral!"

*They were all laying brick.*

Which one of these bricklayers are you today? Which bricklayer do you choose to be this week? If the answers are not the same, you may have a crack to fill.

Part 2: Diving In

# 7
# Be Happy and Content with Yourself and Your Life

*The good ole days weren't always good.*

**—Billy Joel, "Keeping the Faith"**

# Dating 101

Do you think someone new wants to hear about how great things were back when and how awful they are now? Will you draw people to you if you are reaching only out of desperation and because you feel empty, not OK, and lonely? No! It is hard to be happy or content when you are comparing. When you are happy, you will naturally be smiling. You will be here "today" with your head and your heart. What a beautiful picture.

Also, being down on yourself and being self-critical is a downer for the people with you. Get over your mistakes . . . history is history and it no longer exists in the present. Accept yourself as you are today and know that you couldn't have gotten where you are without your history, good or bad. Now go for a new way of life and create it just as you want it to be. Think of yourself as an artist with a blank palette.

In the book *The Artist's Way,* the author suggests an "Artist Date" once a week. I am suggesting a self-date everyday. Play and have fun just for the fun of it. The one you will convince that life is OK is you.

Part 2: Diving In

# 8
# Ask Yourself if You Are Seeing Clearly

*If you want to know your past, look into your present conditions. If you want to know your future, look into your present actions.*

—**Buddha**

## Dating 101

**W**hat would you think about a car that had the front windshield painted black? The only way to see out of the car would be by the rear view mirror, so you could see where you had been but not where you were going. Crazy? Yes, but how many of us live our lives in the past, thinking how much better things were, thinking "if only I would have done things differently," or wishing we could go back?

Stop. By living in the past, we miss the present and how good it can be. The past is over, anyway, and sometimes it wasn't as good as we remember it. It's great to have memories, but not to live in the past.

Is it time to clean off your windshield?

One of the primary reasons it is so difficult for most people to see others clearly is that the person looking is not clearly seeing the person being looked for. Let me give you an example of this. Let's say you are on a first date with someone you met on the Internet. The two of you have corresponded quite a bit and have spent some time on the phone. You like this person and are very excited about meeting him or her. This one may be the one . . . you are almost sure this is the one. You have been lonely and

## Part 2: Diving In

you really want a relationship.

Do you think you will see your date clearly? Not a chance. Your built-up expectations, your impressions from interactions over the phone and e-mail, and your own desire to be in a relationship will get in the way. Your hope that this person is "the one" will inevitably affect what you see in him or her. If by some chance you do penetrate through the excitement of the first date to see glimpses of the real person, you will likely ignore what you are seeing in order to live out the fantasy you have created in your head.

The key to being able to see people clearly is to put yourself aside completely, to get out of the way completely. I don't mean that you go on a date and only let the other person talk, or that you hide yourself. I do mean that in order to see people clearly, you will need to learn how to silence your internal dialogue by handling the expectations and fears caused by self-limiting beliefs and needs.

You may not think you have any internal dialogue, expectations, fears, self-limiting beliefs, needs, or fantasies, but understand that all of us have a constantly running internal dialogue. It's how we process all the experiences the world sends us. In that inside dialogue, life stressors, self-esteem issues, negative self-talk, expectations, fears, self-limiting beliefs, needs, and fantasies play a large part all of the time. It's a part of human experience. This is why meditation and prayer are staples of all major religions. They are spiritual methods of guiding that internal dialogue and helping us be less preoccupied so that we may be present to the divine.

To silence your internal dialogue may seem like a daunting task, one you may not think you need or want to do. I assure you, you will not be able to get to know or see people clearly without learning how to "get out of the way." So, how do you do that?

Here is one key: since your internal dialogue is an internal process, and you are bigger than your internal experiences and processes, you can be the master of it. You can learn how to turn down the volume inside your head and how to have peace. This is a learned skill that comes as you practice understanding yourself and your internal dynamics.

**Part 2: Diving In**

# 9

# Remember, First Dates Are Just a Moment in Time

*It's just a date—not the rest of your life.*

**—Dee Frazier**

## Dating 101

Don't spend hours fantasizing or getting yourself wound up in expectations. Remember that, most often, a first date is a time to decide if you want a second date. Let it be simple.

Now the next part—you have had a great date, and now the wondering and the brain horror begins: Will he/she call? If I call, will I be rejected? Your internal dialogue goes from fantasizing to obsessing.

**Part 2: Diving In**

# 10

# Stop the Buzzing in Your Brain

*Someone who doesn't make flowers makes thorns.
If you're not building rooms where wisdom can
be openly spoken, you're building a prison.*

**—Rumi, from *Say I Am You***

## Dating 101

Immediately after the great first date, start planning other things to do. Fill your calendar and know you can always change plans if you get (and want) a next date. Get involved with other people and things that you would like to do. Do not sit by the phone. Remember, you were also responsible for the first great date and you can create that again and again.

**Part 2: Diving In**

# 11
# Be Authentic and Honest

*To thine own self be true. Thou canst not then be false to any man.*

**—Shakespeare**

## Dating 101

I have read countless books about dating, all full of rules about what to say and not to say. But the truth is simply this: be kind, compassionate, honest, and natural.

We are far more transparent then we would like to believe. People can sense when we are phony or trying to "act" right.

Be willing to stand tall, project confidence and have an open mind and heart as you welcome people, events, and life. Remember, your mother always told you to "stand up straight." Check yourself in the mirror, create the posture that suits you the best, and practice it always.

**Part 2: Diving In**

# 12

# Do Not Take Rejection Personally

*Rejection is protection.*

—**Barbara Graham, PhD**

## Dating 101

So, Mr. Right doesn't call you back after the third date. Who cares? Get right back out there again.

So Ms. Right doesn't give you her phone number the first time you ask her. What does that really mean?

It's only a date—not the rest of your life.

**Part 2: Diving In**

# 13

# Conquer Fear of Rejection

*The way I see it, if you want the rainbow, you gotta put up with the rain.*

**—Dolly Parton**

## Dating 101

Do say "Next!" Any good salesperson knows "yes," "no," and "next." Rejection is not personal.

Learn to say "Next." Then try, try again.

Practice saying: "That was good practice." Remember to say to yourself: "I'm wonderful, I'm smart, and I never, ever give up."

Let rejection fuel you, because if it doesn't fuel you, it will drain you. Ask yourself after every rejection how you will do even better the next time, and use the disappointment to project you toward that moment. Rejection is seldom about you. It is usually a reflection of the other person, so let it stay there. Learn from every rejection, but don't take them on as baggage.

Part 2: Diving In

# 14

# Design Your New Wardrobe

*What we are selling, in everything we do, is ourselves. Your image sets the tone of all your encounters and can have a subtle, yet deep impact. The clothing you wear has a psychological effect on how others respond to you.*

—**Catherine Hatcher, author of the audio CD *Image Matters . . . Creating A Successful Image* and owner of Personas Image Dynamics.**

# Dating 101

A wonderful client of mine became single after a long marriage, a marriage that had lost its passion a long time ago. Often when that happens, each person loses the zest and passion for life and living. Now it's time to get out, look the part, liven up, and have sexual energy.

When she went to her closet, all she saw were "married pants, married shirts, and married shoes." You know what I mean . . . drab, boring . . . like the life she had left. When we went on our first outing together to a charity ball (a wonderful place to meet interesting people), she bought an inexpensive gown that was perfect and we picked out the best earrings for her beautiful face. Well, it was a miracle right before my eyes.

This woman was transformed into a dynamic, sensual, happy, glowing female who was ready to enter a brand new adventure. Sometimes all it takes is new earrings, a new hairstyle, or new sexy underwear. (Extremely sexy underwear feels great.)

This works for men, too. Oh, and guys, it's OK to dye your hair if you want to.

## Part 2: Diving In

I coached a beautiful female physician who felt that she had to look professional all the time. Of course, that "look" was in her mind only. She thought she had to have a clinical external appearance, one that was unattractive, not feminine.

Avoid these appearance turnoffs at all costs:

- A hairdo that is fixed too tightly.
- Tight pants or panty lines.
- An overdose of perfume (men and women).
- Heavy gold chains on men.
- T-shirts with names on them.
- Sweaters with reindeer.
- Leg warmers, except for dance lessons.
- Multi-colored suspenders.

# Dating 101

A makeover is not just makeup and a new outfit. It's about changing style and losing a few pounds. Men now go to hairdressers for the right style. It's about coming out, "single-ing," and being the best you can be.

Consult an image specialist or tell your hairdresser that you want the "latest and greatest" hairstyle.

Nothing boosts your ego better then a flurry of compliments and activity because you are seen in a different way.

Remember all the "before" and "after" commercials? Well, the reason they are so popular is that we like the transformation. Get your teeth whitened, change your hairdo, and go for a complete makeover where it is needed. The caterpillar is becoming the butterfly.

Part 2: Diving In

# 15

# Direct Your New Healthy Lifestyle

*Let your food be your medicine and medicine be your food.*

—**Hippocrates**

## Dating 101

You knew this was coming. Eat healthy, exercise regularly, and get plenty of sleep. Sounds like the same advice that you get for your entire life's journey. Sometimes after a divorce or when our self-esteem is low, we forget those simple rules and indulge ourselves in the wrong things.

Take a good hard look at yourself with honest introspection—no excuses. Face yourself head-on and change the behaviors that are keeping you from feeling great.

Eliminate all addictive habits, and create a daily regime of exercise. If you have any physical problems, start slowly and get advice from an expert as to the best type of movement for the best results for you.

## Part 2: Diving In

Consult a nutritionist or buy a great book—not about diet, but about eating healthfully. If you need to lose some weight, get started right now in a very sensible way. Not only will you look better, but you will feel better, which will make you look better. Get it?

Breathing is a good thing. It sounds funny, but lots of people walk around holding their breath or doing very shallow breathing. Learn breathing techniques and practice. Oxygen is good for your complexion and your general well being.

Sitting still and being with self—taking deep breaths—is very refreshing and replenishes the soul.

Dating 101

# 16
# Let Your Friends Help

*It is not so much our friends' help that helps us as the confident knowledge that they will help us.*

**—Epicurus**

## Part 2: Diving In

Friends, friends, and more friends. The definition of a friend is someone with whom you have the inexpressible comfort of feeling safe and having neither to weigh thoughts nor measure words.

It is also important to have good friends of the opposite sex. (They can give you great perspective.)

Many years ago when I went to my first "singles' party," I went over to a woman who was alone. I sat down, introduced myself, and told her I was new on the singles' scene. She proceeded to tell me all the terrible possibilities that would be available to me as a newly divorced single woman. I understood why she was sitting alone!

Fortunately, that same evening I met another woman and she said, "Great! I will have a brunch at my home and invite some people for you to meet." She and I became friends and did lots of single things together. She knew "the ropes" and was very glad to fill me in.

# Dating 101

After my divorce, most of my friends were still married, and since we were living in the area that my last husband was from, initially they were mostly "his" friends. I needed friends. We all do.

There is all kinds of "support" out there. Go to the places that have the things you like to do or that you might want to learn. For instance, if you want to dance, go to the social clubs that give lessons or encourage single people to attend alone.

Almost every type of organization—from Toastmasters to Safari Clubs, to arts and science clubs—has a singles organization as part of it. Consider attending houses of worship, community centers, and/or theatre groups. Volunteer for charitable groups or political campaigns. The list is endless. If you live in a big city there will be notices in the local paper as to what's going on around town for singles, and sometimes the organizations indicate the age range of group participants.

## Part 2: Diving In

Oh, did I mention? You can start your own group.

If you are in a small city, you might have to go directly to the organization and ask. Do ask.

On another note, check out perspective dates and relationships with friends. Very often the restrooms of a dance lounge or any event are a great place to ask, "What do you think of him/her?" "Do you know anything about them?" I have done that lots of times, and many, many people have asked me the same.

I remember years ago there was a man who had been somewhat abusive to his dates, and I will tell you, this tidbit went through the group like wildfire. That's a good thing.

Part 3: Learning Dating Tactics

# Part 3: Learning Dating Tactics

Dating 101

# 1

# Have Fun with Flirting!

*Flirting is a playful form of communication that acknowledges another human being and expresses interest such that the opposite party can respond verbally or non-verbally to indicate a desire to meet.*

## —Julie Overholt, Professional Certified Coach

# Part 3: Learning Dating Tactics

Effective flirting is simply a way to let people know that you noticed them and want to get to know them. Nothing more and nothing less. Keep it light and keep it fun.

In fact, FLIRT . . . FLIRT . . . FLIRT!

> *Learn to flirt and not look like you are in heat!*
>
> **—Susan Bradley**

The most effective flirting always includes a smile and eye contact.

Flirting is not a serious pastime. Right? It is a fun activity that everyone should engage in from time to time and thoroughly enjoy. When you take the fun out of flirting, it becomes a high-stress situation that has nothing to do with enjoying yourself. Keep it low pressure, just like dating. Flirting should be all fun and games.

Flirting is about right now . . . in the moment . . . no long-term agenda attached . . . no goals. It really is a gift that you give someone. Give for the gift of giving.

# Dating 101

If you are stuck with "nice girls don't flirt," get over it. And guys, don't forget that if you flirt right, it is appropriate behavior.

A clue for the ladies: men are not used to women flirting and there is no question that they would love to be approached first. Go for it! Look over your shoulder and flirt . . . WOW! That will do it every time.

Flattery is to flirting what a match is to dynamite. And use lots of energy in your, "Hello!"

I give a look that says, "I want to know you better." Lots of times, a man has stopped by to talk because I smiled and let him know I was interested in him as a person.

Here are a few don'ts: don't tease, don't cling, don't fidget and don't make a big deal about it—have fun!!

Remember: eye contact is not staring.

**Part 3: Learning Dating Tactics**

# 2

# Take Cues

*Knowledge has never been known to enter
the head via an open mouth.*

**—Anonymous**

# Dating 101

When approaching people, take cues as to where they are in their life right now. Some newly single people will be sensitive to body language that they don't understand. On an evening out some years ago I was with a newly divorced friend and I introduced her to one of my men friends. He joined us and immediately acted as though he and she had the same relationship and friendship that he and I had fostered over many years. She didn't understand it and felt "hovered over" and left early.

My advice to him at the time was to act as though she were not introduced but were a stranger with whom he attempted to elicit a conversation. He should take the cues from her as to what is acceptable for her now. The confusion was the mutual friendship between the man and me, but she became immediately uncomfortable. It actually was a boundary issue that he needed to be aware of.

**Part 3: Learning Dating Tactics**

# 3

# Be Careful with Your Opinions

*It's what you learn after you know it all that counts.*

**—John Wooden**

## Dating 101

Be careful about your opinions. When you are meeting people and getting to know them, it is important that you express yourself honestly; however, opinions are just that—opinions. Many opinions are based on your judgment and can be misconstrued and sound insulting. A perfect example would be: "You look great tonight. I like this outfit much better then the one you wore the other night." I actually had someone say that to me and it took me back. I didn't know if I should have said, "Thank you," had a comeback, or simply let it go. Be generous with your sincere compliments and forget the criticism. You don't have the right.

Speaking of opinions, the best advice is to avoid the three C's—criticizing, condemning, and complaining. When you are meeting a group for the first time, don't jump in and begin to monopolize the conversation with questions that go on and on. Don't ask: "What is your favorite book, magazine, TV show, etc.?" then wait for the answer so that you can give a five-minute dissertation on your thoughts on the matter. I know you know what I mean—this type of conversation has happened to all of us. Be careful you aren't the one who does it.

## Part 3: Learning Dating Tactics

# 4
# Avoid Mind Reading

*The imagination is far more powerful than the will.*

**—Peter Daniels**

# Dating 101

For many people, dating is an exercise in mind reading. Do you know what I mean?

When you are starting to date someone, isn't your mind busy analyzing your date's every action? "Does he like me?" "What does she mean by that?" "Will he call again?" "Did I say the right thing or will she take it wrong?" "Will he reject me or judge me?" "How does she really feel?" "What does he really want?"

The funny thing is that most people don't admit to believing in psychics and mind readers, and yet they try to read minds when we are dating.

Mind reading seldom, if ever, works. It is simply not possible to accurately interpret another person's actions, thoughts, and feelings without input from them. Mind reading can lead you down the wrong road about your new relationship and will definitely drive you crazy.

# Part 3: Learning Dating Tactics

Are you ready to stop driving yourself crazy by trying to figure out another person's thoughts, feelings, and emotions? Then it's time to welcome a new life with fewer headaches, more sleep, and more pleasant dating through communication.

All you have to do is assume it's not personal and communicate.

In mind reading, you would assume that another's actions are a direct reflection of what the person thinks and feels about you. The truth is that even when you are in a long-term relationship, very little of your partner's actions have to do with you. This is even more profoundly so in dating situations.

What the other person is doing or saying, or not doing or saying, has very little to do with you and a lot to do with his or her life experiences, way of being, and current circumstances.

# Dating 101

If he or she is rigid or uncomfortable, it may have very little to do with you. It could just as easily be because he or she does not do first conversations well, or is feeling unattractive, overwhelmed, and anxious, etc. If he or she ends a first date early, it could be that you were not the right person, or it could be that negative emotions just got the best of him or her. Even if ultimately the person you went out with does not choose to date you, that choice is about him or her and is not a comment on your date-worthiness.

Communicate! In mind reading, you will respond to another according to your interpretation of his or her actions. The other person will, in turn, respond to you according to his or her interpretation of your actions, and so on.

Without mind reading and hence interpretation, the logical step is to communicate. Ask questions. Share your feelings. Ask for what you want. Expand your communication repertoire. As long as you are gentle and respectful, you can say almost anything to anyone without causing an adverse reaction.

# Part 3: Learning Dating Tactics

Communicating instead of mind reading will open the door to new understandings and new connections. You will from time to time meet someone who resists participating in an open and flowing conversation, but this resistance is rooted in what's going on in the other person's life and is not about you.

When you play the mind-reading game, you set yourself up for craziness and often for disappointment, resentment, fear, and anxiety. Once you stop playing the game, realize what's going on with the other person is not personal, and start communicating, you'll notice a dramatic change in your peace of mind and the quality of your dating experience.

Women and men, as they get older, allow their cumulative experience with the opposite sex to cloud their view of others as individuals.

Dating 101

# 5
# Be Approachable

*He has the personality of a dial tone.*

—**Phyllis Diller**

# Part 3: Learning Dating Tactics

*Some people are so nervous they keep the coffee awake at night.*

**—Anonymous**

This is my favorite subject. I have gotten more compliments from my willingness to smile at a stranger. It's the best form of flirting because there is nothing attached to the smile, except a genuine feeling of friendliness.

When you are dancing, dining, shopping, or sitting at the local coffee shop, turn on the smile and keep smiling. Even if you're smiling at no one! Your conscience likes it, too. You can fool yourself into a good mood by smiling.

I was dancing with some friends one evening, and a man came over to me and said he loved watching me dance because I was happy and smiling. He said he always wanted to take Argentine tango lessons and would love to have me dance as his partner for the lessons. What a gift.

I gave him my card and he called a few days later and again said he wanted a happy dance partner. He was new in town and felt that a lot of people were not approachable, but he knew I would be.

# 6
# Dance Your Way to New Friends and Fitness

*Nothing gives such complete and profound happiness as the perpetually fresh wonder and mystery of exciting life.*

—**Norman Vincent Peale**

## Part 3: Learning Dating Tactics

Imagine meeting potential dating material while salsa dancing or doing the mambo. People love to socialize while they swing and sway, and dancing is a great way to stay in shape and connect with new people.

Taking group dance lessons or joining a dance club is fulfilling and great for your social life. Moving to the beat and learning new steps is satisfying in itself, and allows you to meet people in a relaxed, nonthreatening setting.

Plus, because of the body language expressed while dancing, you can usually tell by the way someone moves if he or she is the romantic type or not.

If you concentrate on your dancing rather than on getting people to like you, chances are you'll look more confident and attractive.

# 7
# Do Have a Quick Comeback

*Watch out for the emergencies. They are your big chance.*

—**Fritz Reiner**

## Part 3: Learning Dating Tactics

Have an answer ready for the line you hate. Also, if someone criticizes you without permission, it is OK to say, "You did not have permission to give your opinion. I am very selective about the people I choose to give me opinions, and you are not one of them." Well, that might sound harsh, but look at it this way: the criticism usually is not constructive and is meant to hurt or have someone else "be right." None of that is appropriate.

I was out one night having a wonderful time with lots of friends. I was wearing a great halter top with a "V" in the front, which was a little revealing. No big deal as far as I was concerned. I began dancing with a man whom I had known for a long time to be a good dancer, but a rather cynical type who "observes" everyone and then gives his opinions. He said to me, "That halter is sexy and classy. You always look sexy, but sometimes it is not classy." Can you imagine? I walked off the dance floor after telling him that I am very selective of the people whose opinions I care about.

Here's my comeback for the question, "Why are you still single?" Are they not asking, "What's wrong with you?" After many answers that felt to me as if I was being defensive, I now just say, "I really don't know. What do you think?"

# 8
# Know Who Pays

*You will like yourself better when you have approval of your conscience.*

**—Orison Scott Marden**

# Part 3: Learning Dating Tactics

The world has changed and so have the rules on dating. Now it is OK to have your own rules; however, I believe that whoever asks, pays. Real simple. Personally, I love to be courted, so my expectations are that the men pay. I have been really very lucky that the men who show up to date me, and there are many, feel the same way.

I reciprocate by getting tickets, cooking dinner (not too often), or making an offer of something unexpected—such as tickets to a ball game, or wine, cheese, and a picnic. I have also been known to receive an invitation to a great party or function and to call a male friend with, "Hello! Get out your tuxedo and escort me to this event!"

A humorous money situation happened to a client who went to dinner with a man. She didn't finish her meal, so he told her that he would take it home and it would be his lunch the next day. He decided that because he paid for dinner, he was entitled to the leftovers. That was their first and last date.

Dating 101

# 9

# Log in to Ads, Dating Services, and Singles Clubs

*I love a broad margin in my life.*

—**Henry David Thoreau**

## Part 3: Learning Dating Tactics

**W**hen you are date shopping, operate out of a sense of abundance, not scarcity. Deliberately increase the flow of people through your life. Logging on is just another way of connecting with people, and when you use good judgment, it can be a wonderful resource.

Here is the story of my "famous Internet date" (and I have had lots of them): I communicated with a man in Florida—Robert. After great phone conversations, I agreed to go visit him. I knew enough about him to feel comfortable that I would be safe. I gave all his contact information to several of my friends and ventured off. On the plane, I sat next to a charming man, and before the trip was over, I knew a great deal about him. I told him what I was up to and asked that he stay with me until I met the man I was going to see. He agreed, mostly because of two things. One, he was intrigued that I had "the nerve" to take this trip, and two, if the Internet date didn't materialize at the airport, we were going to go dancing that night.

He walked with me down the escalator and there was Robert, standing across the lobby.

## Dating 101

Well, it didn't turn out to be any more than a nice trip, and that was that. Nothing ventured, nothing gained, and I did have a whirlwind weekend with Robert in a great part of the country.

I went to a dinner party with my youngest daughter, who is single and does a lot of Internet dating. At the party was a woman who was quite negative.

She was talking about a friend of hers who she thought was "really stupid" for believing a story that an Internet date had told her. She said, "Can you imagine that she believes that this guy has a plane, travels all over, has a lot of money, and would like to fly into town and treat her royally?" She went on and on about her feelings about her friend being gullible and being misled.

Suddenly my daughter said, "What is his name? I think I dated him." It was hysterical. My daughter Cheryl was being honest and wasn't intending to put the woman down. She was innocently curious, but her question did the trick. This is a perfect example of different spins on the same subject.

**Part 3: Learning Dating Tactics**

# 10

# Keep the Spark...Be in the Moment

*People are like stained glass windows. They sparkle and shine when the sun is out, but when the darkness sets in, their true beauty is revealed only if there is a light within.*

**—Elisabeth Kübler-Ross**

## Dating 101

It's easy to shine when you get out of your own way. Stop paying attention to the "shoulds" other people are so quick to share. Pay attention instead to the truth that is you—your inner wisdom and beauty.

Part 3: Learning Dating Tactics

# 11
# Be Fully Yourself

*We must be trying to learn who we really are rather than telling ourselves who we should be.*

**—Father John Powell, SJ**

# Dating 101

No matter how "good" or "bad" you think you may be, relish the day when the *National Enquirer* makes that pronouncement and you are laughing on the beach in Tahiti. You are neither good nor bad. You just are. Some will love you, some won't. It doesn't matter. And who cares what others really think, anyway? If you are living in your truth, your life is perfect!

When I first got in the seminar business and began coaching people about thirty years ago, I had to learn that lesson very quickly. Some people will love you, and some will think you aren't so great. If you "show up" every single time, the odds are in your favor. Just be pleased with yourself.

# Part 3: Learning Dating Tactics

# 12

# Get Seen, Get Heard

*If opportunity doesn't knock, build a door.*

—**Milton Berle**

## Dating 101

Get seen and get heard in as many places as possible, as frequently as you can. When somebody realizes that special quality they are looking for, we want your face right in front of them! You have a unique gift. If you keep it a secret, you'll never be "discovered." Let people know who you are.

I always advise my clients to keep going to things that interest them. Stay out there, be available, participate, and contribute to everything that you touch in your life, and sooner or later the payback will be exactly what you want.

**Part 3: Learning Dating Tactics**

# 13

# Be Persistent

*Most people give up just when they're about to achieve success. They quit on the one yard line. They give up at the last minute of the game, one foot from a winning touchdown.*

**—H. Ross Perot**

## Dating 101

Remember, this whole experience of being single again is new. You may not get it the way you want it to be right off the bat. Keep getting out. Keep honing in on your skills to find yourself in the perfect relationship. Keep in mind that happiness is a way of travel, not a destination.

**Part 3: Learning Dating Tactics**

# 14
# Develop a Thick, Yet Removable, Skin

*We don't see things as they are. We see them as we are.*

**—Anais Nin**

## Dating 101

Your public will adore you or abhor you based on the quality of their lives, not yours. Keep your creative heart accessible while making mental boundaries about what you will not let affect you. What other people think and say about you is none of your business. Stay true to yourself. It is the only thing that matters.

**Part 3: Learning Dating Tactics**

# 15
# Emulate the Greatest (to a Point)

*One man practicing sportsmanship is far better than fifty preaching it.*

**—Knute K. Rockne**

## Dating 101

Imitate the strategies your friends have used that have worked, while keeping your identity firmly rooted in Number One! If someone else has done it, so can you. Find the model, learn the strategies, and then implement them in your own life.

**Part 3: Learning Dating Tactics**

# 16
# Entertain Yourself

*If you want to make good use of your time, you've got to know what's most important and then give it all you've got.*

**—Lee Iacocca**

## Dating 101

Keep finding more new ways to entertain yourself. Hey, if you don't find yourself interesting, who else will? Life is full of wonderful and exciting adventures. Explore. Experiment. LIVE!

**Part 3: Learning Dating Tactics**

# 17
# Build a Community

*Give the world the best you have and the best will come back to you.*

—**Madeline Bridges**

## Dating 101

Build a community of your raving fans. How do you do this? Easily! Add a lot of value to others in whatever way comes naturally to you. Raving fans sing your praises without your having to do anything more than be yourself. Treat people the way you want to be treated. Smile more. Praise people. Acknowledge others a lot! Give of yourself, your time, your energy, and your love. People are hungry for your attention and they will remember you. Then they'll talk about you.

**Part 3: Learning Dating Tactics**

# 18

# Think of the Date as an Interview... Sort Of

*Have a well-stocked briefcase.*

**—Dee Frazier**

# Dating 101

In all my years coaching people through their career changes, I have always encouraged my clients to go on interviews that could lead to potentially good positions. I told them not to prejudge the offer or the results of an interview, but to go with an open mind and an open heart and to be available for the possibility that the position would be perfect. You always have a choice as to whether you want a "second interview." I remember people being fearful of going on an interview because they might get an offer for a position they didn't want. Many newly singles have that same fear. What will I do if I get asked out and don't want to go?

Now, remember that on an interview, especially when both parties are qualifying and getting comfortable, no person should ask questions like, "What are the benefits of this relationship?" As the dating process progresses, there will be opportunities to ask more personal, intimate questions. Not until the dating process becomes a relationship is it OK to ask personal or intimate questions.

When the interview process gets down to the negotiating stage (is this relationship about to form?), then the conversation can go towards, "What's in it for me?"

# Part 3: Learning Dating Tactics

First date? Try these appropriate questions:

- What do you do?
- Where do you live?
- How do you like your job?
- Are you married? (Even before the date—very important!)
- What do you like to do in your spare time?

First date inappropriate questions:

- How much money do you make?
- How old are you?
- Do you want to get married?
- Why are you still single?

# Dating 101

- Now all that being said, I know that people will hate the word "interview" because they really don't want to be interviewed. To a certain extent, I am one of those persons; however, considering the first date an "interview" helps guide people who are just starting out in the single world. So let's call it "interview-lite" and not "interrogation."

**Part 3: Learning Dating Tactics**

# 19

# Use the Magic of "No"

*Our lives are a sum total of the choices we have made.*

—**Dr. Wayne Dyer**

# Dating 101

You have the right to say NO whenever you want the interaction to stop. That includes first dates, second dates, sex, or anything else that you don't want to participate in. It's amazing, but some people don't know that they can (and often should) say no.

**Part 3: Learning Dating Tactics**

# 20
# Accept Compliments

*You never know when a moment and a few sincere words can have an impact.*

—**Zig Ziglar**

**Dating 101**

Give compliments often and generously. Be careful not to compliment things that you don't believe are true because the other person will know. Compliments validate other people. You are telling them that you noticed, and that something about them was interesting.

**Part 3: Learning Dating Tactics**

# 21

# Be Playful

*At the height of laughter, the universe is flung into a kaleidoscope of new possibilities.*

**—Jean Houston**

# Dating 101

The best thing you can be out there is playful and fun. When I am playful I know that my sexual energy is really out there—not to seduce or manipulate, but to attract "playmates." Get comfortable with your sexuality and you will find yourself feeling more attractive and confident.

**Part 3: Learning Dating Tactics**

# 22

# Look for Friends, Not Lovers

*Friendship is like vitamins: we supplement each other's minimum daily requirements.*

## —Kathy Mohnke

# Dating 101

Remember: It's just a date—not the rest of your life! If you keep adding to your list of the criteria for the perfect date, you are probably being too exclusive and will exclude a lot of people with whom you could have had a great exchange. I find that men do this more than women. They have a list of what a woman has to look like—size, shape, face, hair color, and on and on and on. I have a male friend who is even concerned about "cup" size. Here are two ways to help you determine if your list is too rigid: (1) you haven't met anyone who meets the criteria, and (2) the list is getting bigger.

Since this isn't about finding a "mate" for life, overlook some of the qualities that you think you cannot live without and forget the list. Have the date and decide whether you want a second date. You might have a ball, and you'll make a friend, which is a great start for any relationship.

Many wonderful relationships start off with a casual beginning. When you first meet someone, you might say "no way" for this reason or that, but before you know it, you aren't even looking and the relationship blossoms. The fun may last for a few weeks or forever. It doesn't matter, as long as you're having fun.

**Part 3: Learning Dating Tactics**

# 23
# Decide Where to Go

*Lead the life that will make you kindly and friendly to everyone about you, and you will be surprised what a happy life you will lead.*

**—Charles M. Schwab**

## Dating 101

**D**o the things that you love to do and meet the people who love to do the same things. I love to dance, so I go to places where there is live music, and I meet lots of men who love to do the same thing. When I travel, I find out where the dance clubs are. Last December, I spent two weeks in Louisville, Kentucky, on a business trip. After the third day there, I discovered the "Derby City Bop Club."

I went to a well-known dance club (some people called it a meat market, but that was only their opinion), and I positioned myself at a table right by the dance floor. I ordered something to eat and a drink and watched the dancers. I very quickly determined who was not coupled and who was a fairly good dancer (I am not into perfection). Since I was a "stranger" to the group, I got lots of looks, but no one asked me to dance.

I picked a man who looked like he could handle being asked, and I went over to him and said, "I am from out of town and don't know anyone. Would you be willing to dance with me?" Very few men could turn down that request.

## Part 3: Learning Dating Tactics

Well, that got the ball rolling. I danced all night with lots of men and then learned all the places to go in Louisville. I danced almost every night for the duration of my stay, and I still get calls from men and women as to when I am coming back. It made my business trip much more enjoyable, to say the least.

What do you like to do? Make a list of your favorite activities, such as:

- Mountain climbing
- Whitewater rafting
- Hiking
- Running, bicycling, water sports
- Visiting museums
- Volunteering for charitable organizations

Dating 101

# 24
# Invite a Friend

*Friendship doesn't make you wealthy, but true friendship will reveal the wealth within you.*

**—Anonymous**

## Part 3: Learning Dating Tactics

Be sure that anyone you invite into a group gets introduced properly and is made to feel comfortable. There was an occasion in which I was brought into a group by a friend who very quickly deserted me so that he could do whatever he wanted. Fortunately, I recovered quickly, introduced myself, and started to connect. For some people, in the beginning that would be more difficult. If you invite a friend, do not abandon him or her. Not only is it good etiquette to stand by your guest's side, but it is also a responsibility that we have to others.

Dating 101

# 25

# Learn and Practice Etiquette

*I may have my faults. But being wrong ain't one of them.*

—**Jimmy Hoffa**

## Part 3: Learning Dating Tactics

**W**hen you feel that you do not want to continue dating, it is not OK to avoid answering the phone because you don't want to reject someone. Write a note or leave a message on his/her answering machine, and state that at this time, you are no longer interested in continuing to date.

A big issue with the forty-five-plus crowd is the opening of doors. We were raised in the generation when the movies always told us that the men opened the doors for the women. Though rules have changed slightly, I still love it. When I am not sure where the man is in his thinking, I will ask: "Would you like me to wait while you open the door?" I promise you they will always say yes. And guys, that is a cue for you so that you know what to do. Remember, mind reading is out. So, to get what you really want in a date, speak the words so the other person gets the information. Never chastise the other person for not doing it the way you want if you haven't even told him or her what you want in the first place!

Never be rude to a waitress or waiter, and—of course—never, ever flirt with someone of the opposite sex while you're on a date.

Dating 101

# 26

# Dos and Don'ts on the First Date

*A mistake only proves someone stopped talking long enough to do something.*

—**Dr. Michael LeBoeuf**

# Part 3: Learning Dating Tactics

I often hear of singles who envision a first date as a way to "size up" their dates instead of as a way to simply get to know and enjoy the other person. Needless to say, those who conduct the first date that way seldom end up on a second date. Why would this be?

Simply put, people desire to be liked and wanted. People want warmth and a person at the other side of the table who is excited about the potential of the meeting. People seldom want to fit into someone else's rigid idea of a perfect mate.

Simply being with the person in a relaxed atmosphere and talking about life should give you enough information to know if that person is not "the one." The key is to trust your gut if you feel a person is not right for you, without having to justify why you may feel that way.

On the other hand, if you end up leaving a relaxed first date unsure of whether or not that person is a good fit, then congratulations—you did it exactly right. Any individual, no matter how simple he or she may seem, cannot be measured by someone else's list of traits for the perfect mate. We, as human beings, are far too complex to be reduced to a list.

Dating 101

# 27

# Consider These Dos and Don'ts of the First Date

*I hated every minute of the training, but I said, "Don't quit. Suffer now and live the rest of your life as a champion."*

**—Mohammed Ali**

## Part 3: Learning Dating Tactics

- Do not have sex on the first date. Sex may sell—but first-date sex sells you short.

- Do K.I.S.S. (Keep It Short and Simple). Leave them wanting more, or leave as soon as possible!

- Be a good listener. Your date is flattered, and you're informed!

- Don't trash-talk your ex. There's a fine line between love and hate, and for guys, passionate hate means, "I'm still not over my ex."

- Don't be an open book. If you want to be a must-read, don't offer up the Cliffs Notes.

- Don't bring up the "M" word (marriage) on the first date. If the other person does, what should you do? Brush it off with your "M" word: "MAYBE . . . someday . . . when I've taken the time to find the right person."

# Dating 101

- Dare to have spares. Dating is a numbers game: the more people you date, the better the odds are of meeting some really good eggs.

- Trust your instincts. If the other person is "creeping you out," take flight. Don't fight your gut feeling.

- Trust in yourself. Your perceptions are often far more accurate than you are willing to believe.

- Think friendship first. If things don't work out, you end up with a new friend who may fix you up with someone who WILL work out.

- DO HAVE FUN! Smiles + laughter = major turn-on!

**Part 3: Learning Dating Tactics**

# 28

# Things to Avoid if You Want a Second Date

*A sense of humor is what makes you laugh at something that would make you mad if it happened to you.*

—**Anonymous**

## Dating 101

- Don't come to the door wearing a wedding gown.

- Don't discuss past significant relationships and tell your current date how you're going to get even with your exes.

- Don't start calling every single day because you miss him/her already.

- Don't take her to Hooters or someplace even more tasteless.

- Don't lecture or try to improve your date.

- Don't ask, "Where is this relationship going?"

## Part 3: Learning Dating Tactics

A client named Russell asked what appeared to be a lovely woman out for a dinner date. When he met her, she asked if he wouldn't mind stopping at the grocery store because she wanted to get some lipstick and powder. He was glad to oblige.

As it turned out, she proceeded to do an entire grocery order and then when they got to the check out, she didn't have any money and had forgotten her checkbook. He was too glad to offer her the loan. He paid for the groceries and they went to dinner.

After that night she didn't take his calls, and of course never paid his money back. NOT OK!!

*You grow up the day you can have your first real laugh—at yourself.*
**—Ethel Barrymore**

**Part 4: Last-Minute Tools for Your Dating Toolbox**

# Part 4: Last-Minute "Tools" for Your Dating Toolbox

## Dating 101

# 1
# Understand Acceptable Flattery Zones

*"Goodness, what beautiful diamonds," remarked a hatcheck girl. "Goodness has nothing to do with it, Dearie."*

—**Mae West**

# Part 4: Last-Minute Tools for Your Dating Toolbox

It's important to know the safe areas for flattering another person. What may seem like flattery to one person can be insulting to another. Again, common sense is important.

Women like to be complimented on their hair style, their eyes, their manicure, and their shoes. In other words, these are safe areas for flattery.

Women do NOT like to be "complimented" on their anatomy, their hair color, their pants, or their makeup, especially in the early stages of dating—and possibly ever, depending on the woman.

The safe flattery areas for men are their neckties, their eyes, their watches, their briefcases, their shoes, and their hair. Do NOT compliment their pants, hairpieces, anatomy, or wallet size.

You get the drift. Use good judgment here.

Dating 101

# 2
# Heed the Dating Red Flags

*Weakness of attitude becomes weakness of character.*

—**Albert Einstein**

## Part 4: Last-Minute Tools for Your Dating Toolbox

Just because you have been out of the dating world for thirty years, you have no excuse to be naïve or gullible.

If you notice any of these "red flags," take heed:

- He can only be reached by cell phone.

- She's not available on weekends.

- He's secretive and won't give straight answers.

- You know little about her past.

- He repeats unfavorable behavior, even after you have asked him to stop.

- She wants to move too fast.

- You catch him in a lie.

# Dating 101

What do you do if you know someone is lying? When I know someone is lying, I view it as entertaining. I don't necessarily feel the need to correct or challenge that person. I will just make the decision not to have a second date. You do not need to "correct" or "coach" that person, just consider it an experience and get on with your life . . . without this person.

Proceed wisely, and when a red flag waves in front of your eyes, thank it for being there.

**Part 4: Last-Minute Tools for Your Dating Toolbox**

# 3

# Dump a Bad Date

*Pain nourishes courage. You can't be brave if you've only had wonderful things happen to you.*

—**Mary Tyler Moore**

# Dating 101

How do you gracefully bow out of the date from hell? Well, all that means is that the date didn't "click." No big deal. Believe it or not, there will be times that you do everything right—you look your best, you've brushed your teeth—and lo and behold you can tell from his/her body language that the connection isn't there.

The bad date will happen. Even Babe Ruth struck out more times than he hit home runs. Sometimes it will not be right because you can't connect or he or she can't connect with you. It's important that you know this might happen. Again, don't take it personally. It's about chemistry—sometimes there is some and sometimes there isn't. I will say it again:

It's just a date—not the rest of your life.

## Part 4: Last-Minute Tools for Your Dating Toolbox

Also, if you are the one who feels that the date is a mistake, be polite, relax, and make the most of the time. If you listen intently—without the mental criticism—you will learn something about yourself and also score points in the area of being a "nice date."

Now if your date is really obnoxious and the person is demonstrating bad behavior, ask to leave or make your own arrangements to leave. Leave if you might be in mental or physical danger.

Here is a tactic I always use in case I anticipate that a date might not be too wonderful. If I am picked up at my home, I carry my garage door opener as well as my keys. That means it isn't necessary to walk me to the door. I just tell the date to pull up to the garage and I jump right out.

Another mantra to repeat over and over again: "I will not live in fear."

Dating 101

# 4

# Choose Dates Who Are the Right Age... For You

*Live your life and forget your age.*

—**Norman Vincent Peale**

## Part 4: Last-Minute Tools for Your Dating Toolbox

Age is a big issue and I hear it all the time. Some women feel that men their age are looking for the cute little blonde to have on their arm, and some women (I am one of them) date mostly younger men.

I think it becomes an issue when someone says, "I will only date younger people." Take this person off your list because he or she has a character issue.

Decide where you are in life: what are your preferences for conversation, maturity, energy, outlook, and values? A person who has the same preferences should be what you look for in the opposite sex. Sometimes older people of both sexes are too set in their ways. So there again, you must be willing to change your outlook, which will improve your sexual vitality. Look "outside the box." Practice being able to attract the perfect date by changing your thinking, not your behavior.

# 5
# Decide Whether or Not to Have Sex

*There may be snow on the roof, but there's a fire blazing in the oven.*

**—Ruth Beckford, from *Still Groovin': Affirmations for Women in the Second Half of Life***

# Part 4: Last-Minute Tools for Your Dating Toolbox

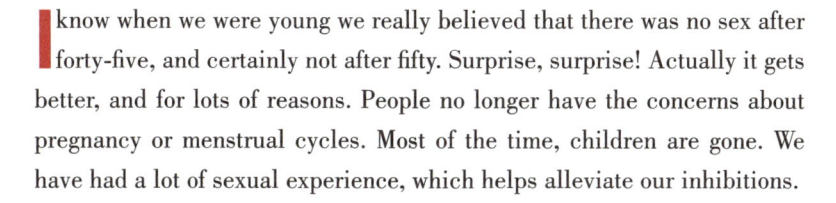

I know when we were young we really believed that there was no sex after forty-five, and certainly not after fifty. Surprise, surprise! Actually it gets better, and for lots of reasons. People no longer have the concerns about pregnancy or menstrual cycles. Most of the time, children are gone. We have had a lot of sexual experience, which helps alleviate our inhibitions.

Also, we have experienced a lot of life's hurts and losses so we know that if the relationship doesn't work out, we will be OK and survive. Knowing we are survivors no matter what opens the door for a much freer sexual experience with a special person.

Rules have changed. Men are no longer considered the assertive ones. Women are getting really clear about what they want and don't want and that includes sex. Recent popular TV shows have made that loud and clear. The characters on the shows may be younger women, but the rules are the same for us.

Being sexy has no age limit. See yourself as sexy . . . have a sexy attitude. No matter what you are wearing, the opposite sex can feel your sexy attitude.

# Dating 101

Treat yourself to a bubble bath and sexy underwear.

Sex does not come with an automatic timer; that is, there is no perfect time to have sex. It depends on you and what you want and if the timing is right for your partner. Allow yourself to experiment and to feel. But remember—playing it safe is a must in today's dating world!

Be really clear about the health issues of casual sex. And don't assume your date is responsible sexually. Like fire, let sex warm you, not burn you.

*When I am good, I am very, very good; but when I am bad, I am better.*
—**Mae West**

One last quick note, primarily for women: On occasion, a man will expect sex as a payback because he has spent some money on dinners, gifts, or entertainment. Sex is not payment for anything . . . sex and lovemaking is for you, and only when you want to.

**Part 4: Last-Minute Tools for Your Dating Toolbox**

# 6

# Knowing What You Are Really Feeling: Is It Love or Just Chemistry?

*A long and happy life lasts five minutes. Happiness is wonderful, but if you have had more than five consecutive minutes of it, it means that you weren't thinking.*

**—Roger Rosenblatt, from *Rules for Aging***

## Dating 101

When you are out on a first date or a first encounter with someone—whether you're on the dance floor or at a party—and all of a sudden you get that feeling from the tip of your head to the bottom of your toes . . . it's chemistry! Lots of sexual energy! Do not mistake this feeling for love or for meeting your soul mate or anything more significant than thinking with "genital intelligence." Enjoy the feeling, but make no decisions based on it.

I have had that happen to me on the dance floor, and the intensity was great. I have even spent the night dancing with the same person and then I never saw him again. That "feeling" is just another moment in time to be savored—nothing more, nothing less.

# Part 4: Last-Minute Tools for Your Dating Toolbox

# 7
# Dance

*Life's a dance you learn as you go.*

—**John Michael Montgomery**

# Dating 101

**W**ell, to me, dancing is romantic, energetic, and playful. Not everyone feels that way. A perfect first date for me would be dinner and dancing.

Let's talk for a minute about meeting people through dancing. It's perfect! Take dance lessons for a dance that you like and one you really want to learn, and you'll find people there who feel the same way. Dancing is very social, so usually a group will go someplace after the lesson, or lots of plans will be made for future dancing.

Dancing creates lively energy. Now, how about dancing on dates?

Be sure that your partner has the same skill level you do or is at least close. Make sure that you choose a dance that is compatible for both of you. Save the jig and jive for another day (not the first date), unless you are sure that this kind of dancing is OK with the other person.

# Part 4: Last-Minute Tools for Your Dating Toolbox

# 8

# Deciding Where to Go Next

*Shoot for the moon—even if you miss,
you'll land among the stars.*

**—Les Brown**

# Dating 101

OK, so what's next? Anything you want is out there. The difference between now and when you were single before is that you have maturity, and you have resolved a lot of "old stuff." Now you are lighter and in a lot of ways more youthful in spirit than when you were in your thirties. You are at a point where change is not so scary . . . your new life appeals to you . . . you are ready to date with enthusiasm, excitement, and a joyful heart.

# Afterword: Living Happily Ever After

*The person who has discovered the pleasures of truly human living, the person whose life is rich in friendships and caring people, the person who enjoys daily the pleasures of good food and sunshine, will not need to wear herself out in pursuit of some other kind of success.*

**—Harold Kushner**

# Dating 101

Where am I today? Every night before going to bed I count my blessings for the wonderful life I have had and for my incredible family.

I commit to living each day with an open heart, and to enjoying the second half of my life. My experiences have caused me to rethink and reexamine my former beliefs, and I know now that I have become a leader for myself and I no longer fear letting other people run my life.

I know that I can love someone openly and enjoy a permanent relationship as I make choices that are healthy, enriching, empowering, and gloriously loving.

As I continue to work on myself, to follow my own tips, and to continue on my own path and purpose, I vow to make a difference in this world and to celebrate the lives of the "baby boomers" who cross my path as they reenter that strange and wonderful world of being single again.

# Afterword

Remember: we all have the power to transform our lives and to find a lifelong, loving partner.

If you are interested in learning more, you can subscribe to my newsletter, published through my company, The University of Dating. Highly trained experts are available to help you plan a wonderful journey as you make the transition back into the world of being single.

My motto is to keep smiling and keep dancing!

*Dee the Dating Diva*

—**"Dee, the Dating Diva" Frazier**
**www.theuniversityofdating.com**

## A PLAN FOR YOUR NEW LIFE

Fill out the following agreement. Tear it out and keep it with you as a reminder of the vow you have taken to improve your life.

## AGREEMENT

I, _____ , understand that I am undertaking a new way of life so I can be happy as a single. I understand that dating should be fun and is only a dance toward a relationship.

I know that change isn't always easy and that the little voice in my head trying to discourage me may not be my friend. I will DISCERN what I listen to.

I, _____ , further understand that emotions and feelings will raise issues for me to deal with. I commit myself to excellent self-care: adequate sleep, diet, exercise, and pampering for the rest of my life.

I, _____ , further commit to the following steps and goals to have fun dating:

1. _____
_____

2. _____
_____

3. _____
_____

4. _____
_____

5. _____
_____

# Dating 101

*It don't mean a thing if it ain't got that swing.*

**—Duke Ellington and Irving Mills**

# Acknowledgments

I wish to acknowledge all my clients who have encouraged me to write this book while they touched my life and allowed me to be part of theirs.

To the three people who have inspired and encouraged me all along the way: Barbara Graham, Nancye Miller, and Laura Lewis. You actually made "The Diva" come to life. My deepest and sincerest gratitude and appreciation for the many hours of "not being sure" and insisting that I do it anyway.

A special thank-you to all my friends who have shared their many thoughts and feelings about relationships. I cherish their friendship and love them deeply. Often in small groups and many times in private conversations they—each and every one—shared openly and honestly from their hearts.

For all of their help with the editing, design, and publication of my book, I would like to thank Milli Brown, Kathryn Grant, Erica Jennings, Deanne Dice, and the rest of the crew at Brown Books Publishing Group.

To my three children, Bruce, Michele, and Cheryl, for being proud and enjoying my success.